My Heart

My Heart in Ink

INNOCENT WHANDE

Thank you for the support. Enjoy the book.

Whande

Copyright

Innocent Whande has asserted his right to be identified as the author of this body of work under the UK's Copyright Act 1988.

No part of this body of work may be reproduced or used in any manner without explicit permission from the author.

Copyright © Innocent Whande 2020

Cover Design: Deon Kearns

Foreword Dr Tom Masters

All rights reserved.

ISBN 9781527275034

Dedication

This book is for my friends, family and everyone who helped me with editing my manuscript, feedback on poems, those I vented to about every process of putting this book together. Those who supported me and encouraged me to keep going. Thank you all for being part of the journey. I appreciate you, enjoy the book.

Foreword

My Heart in Ink is the debut poetry collection by Zimbabwean poet, Innocent Whande. The book transforms personal experience into something of wider cultural/political relevance, asking searching questions about what it means to exist between worlds and how this has impacted his identity. With a collection of poems, the sequencing of individual pieces is very important. They need to speak to each other and ideally create a whole that's greater than the sum of its parts. This approach is effectively used in *My Heart in Ink*.

Innocent succeeds in enhancing his use of metaphor and simile, something that helps to deepen his work and further its emotional impact. Poems such as, 'Gogo's House', for example, paint a vivid portrait of Zimbabwean life, allowing the reader to experience this environment through the poet's eyes. The repetition of 'night' in the penultimate stanza is lyrically effective, and the final stanza (withdrawing into the house, into folktales, and then into prayers before sleep) presents the reader with a powerful and satisfying ending. It also provides an excellent segue into the next poem, 'Dear Lord', which begins with the language of prayer ('Dear Lord, why have you forsaken my people?').

Frequently the poems spark off each other, creating a cumulative understanding of the writer's poetic persona and the experiences that have helped to define it. The 'Dear' poems provide a successful counterpoint to the other pieces in the collection and are most successful when placed at strategic intervals.

There is great use of juxtaposition. The weight of heavy pieces, such as 'Foreigner', is thrown in relief by the likes of 'Dear Phone', something that helps to magnify their respective qualities. Additionally, the use of dry humour in poems like 'Where Are You From?' helps to sharpen their social criticism.

Contents

GOGO'S HOUSE	1
DEAR LORD	2
ANGRY SKIES	3
HOME	4
WHERE ARE YOU FROM?	5
FOREIGNER	6
GREENER PASTURES	8
DEAR STEP COUNTRY	9
GREAT ZIMBABWE	10
DEAR PHONE	11
DEAR FOOD	12
DEAR MUSIC	13
DEAR CRUSH	14
DEAR MAMA	15
DEAR FUTURE DAUGHTER	16
FOOL	18

IF I WERE YOU	19
HEARTACHE	20
I LOVED YOU ONCE	21
ADULTING	22
I LOST MYSELF	23
FORMER SELF	24
DEAR YOU	25
IN SILENCE	26
SURVIVAL	27
LISTEN	28
NEVER FORGOTTEN	29
DEAR UNCLE	30
DEAR SEKURU	31
AUTHOR BIOGRAPHY	33
REFERENCE	34

Author's Note

I am proud to introduce to you, *My Heart in Ink* my debut poetry collection. It feels wonderful to finally publish my poems, after talking about it for so long. The poems will explore my journey through life, the good, bad and the funny.

My hope is that my poems will resonate with you in some way. Some of the poems will make you cry, laugh and there are some thought provoking ones too. This is my calling card to the world; I hope you enjoy reading.

Gogo's House

To the right tucked in a corner
a polished store veranda glistens from a distance
the gate opens into the driveway
trees giving you shade as you park
the house beige in colour
in the right light it looks like it's dripping honey

Everyone is welcome with open arms
an embrace that warms your heart

The house is too hot to sit inside
doors and windows are wide open to let in the cool air
waiting for the temperature to drop when the sun sets
Under the shade of the mango trees we wait out the heat
the sun sets in the distance- taking all the light with it
a crescent moon rises in its place

A breeze sweeps across the land
refreshing us even for a moment
a coke bottle fresh out of the fridge drips with water
music to my ears when it takes a breath as it is popped open
fresh buns straight out of the oven
taking the first bite sends tingles down my spine
the first sip leaves the drink dancing on my tongue

Critters start their chorus and continue through the night
the cattle sound their calls as they retreat for the night
fierce boerbels stand guard and bark at anything that moves

As the night ages we retreat into the house
we share laughs and make fond memories
to bless the night- we pray before we sleep

Dear Lord

Dear Lord- why have you forsaken my people?
nothing grows on our land anymore
the sun destroys the little we can grow
dried up wells leave us with very little water

Our leaders are doing little to help us
they squander a lion's share of our resources
leaving us nothing but crumbs

We used to have bountiful harvests
now we must import even the basics
relying on the goodwill of other nations

The cracked earth bares no food anymore
the scorching sun leaves us withered and weary
the ground feels like walking on embers
the grass shrivelled and stiff like thorns

The fruits have aged on the outside
on the inside they are bitter and dry
even the birds have stopped singing
we grow weary in this barren land

Angry Skies

Heavy downpour descends upon the land
brings with it renewed hope
some new life
or so it seems

It rains as if it's a plague
the wind that comes with it uproots anything in its way
it travels downhill at an alarming pace
houses are sinking
people are swept away by the current
those fortunate enough
find shelter to wait it out
some aren't so lucky

The cries for help are drowned by the unforgiving tide
roads crumble and the earth swallows
all that is in sight
lives are lost
bystanders watch helplessly
rescue attempts are to no avail
the forces of nature are too strong
families are left with nothing but the clothes on their back
their tears are washed away in the rain

Home

When I close my eyes- I can picture home in all its glory
the dusty roads that led to the quaint township
where we stopped on long journeys
local music playing
people dancing on the store verandas
the roaring sound of lorries speeding past

When the buses pulled away a cloud of dust
would linger in the air
people packed on buses like fish
you would be lucky to get both your cheeks on the seat
the roads weren't the kindest either- you had potholes
that could drown a bus

The sun was so hot you could roast maize in it
even the ground felt like you were walking on embers
the best place to be would be under the shed of a tree
sipping on a cold drink- coupled with a bun

You should be there when the crops are near harvest
driving across the country you see a land full of life
Lush green crops occupy the land everywhere you look

Sweet aroma of roasted peanuts and maize linger in the air
ripe fruits causing a lip biting sensation
sizzling steaks on the braai leave you salivating
paired together with glistening fried collard greens
in a medley with juicy tomatoes and onions
completed with the perfectly cooked and steamy sadza
the perfect meal

Where Are You From?

I take my favourite seat at the back of the bus- as usual
earphones on- leaning on the window- taking in the view
lush trees throughout the route
the bus is relatively empty

A middle-aged gentleman gets on- walks to the back
and sits across from me
he mouths something- I take my earphones
out to hear it again

Sorry are you talking to me?
Yes mate- you alright?
I'm good thanks.

Cool cool- so where are you from?
I'm from Brighton.
But where are you really from?
You know- as in your roots
Brighton.

Foreigner

Moving across the world in search for a better life
thousands of miles away from home
my life uprooted in an instant

I find myself getting stares from every passer-by
unwelcomed glares are all I get in this foreign land
rough replies come my way when I ask anything
I learn to enjoy my cluelessness
silence becomes my closest acquaintance

"Go back where you came from"- is implied but never said
you learn to grin and bear it
If you complain you are ungrateful- so you keep it in
you die a little inside with each day
you smile just to mask the pain

You grow fond of your new home
adopting their customs as if they were your own
you get a pat on the back for 'speaking English so well'
the false validation clouds your mind
you've lost who you used to be
you start to struggle to speak your native tongue

You get stopped and searched because
apparently- you fit the description
black and out of place
you get called names
constantly close to tears
if you lash out you are the one who gets in trouble

You go 'home' for a visit
just to be somewhere familiar

everyone wants to hear your 'English accent'
you are just a prop to them now
all you want to do is be your old self again- but you can't
you play the part
once again you grin and bear it

At 'home' you are now a foreigner too
you are torn between two worlds
which one should you be?

Greener Pastures

One day I was in a queue for my visa
next thing I know
I was saying goodbye to everyone and everything I knew
it never clicked until I arrived at the airport

I was about to move across the world
leaving the country for the first time
not knowing what was instore on the other side

My heart sank as I saw my relatives' wave
my brothers and I goodbye

I smiled and laughed
as if we weren't about to leave everything
and everyone we ever knew
no tears in sight- you would think I was a robot

Embracing my mum upon arrival was surreal
I couldn't believe how crowded the place was
the packed shops- lights- sounds and noise everywhere
the likes of which I had only seen on TV
I was in awe

Our mother wanted better for us
She plucked us from all we knew
in search of greener pastures

Dear Step Country

You welcomed me with open arms
I let my guard down
thinking you were different from the others

Some of your children welcomed me
with empty smiles and cold hearts
they muttered insults under their breath
I don't know what I did to deserve that

Some of your children welcomed me with love
made me feel at home
they restored my faith in humanity
they taught me the lay of the land
I can't eat your food though
it doesn't taste real
like it's grown in a lab
Oh- wait
Never mind

All these years I've been here
I can never get used to your ever-changing weather
forever throwing tantrums
Please have a word with Management

Great Zimbabwe

I'm from a stunning place called Zimbabwe
A place where the sun's power can only be matched
by a cold drink
whose sights will take your breath away
from Victoria Falls- Mosi-oa Tunya that will leave you in awe
the stunning scenery from Bvumba mountains
the breath-taking Matopo hills
the mystical Chinhoyi caves
the majestic Great Zimbabwe

You are spoilt for choice wherever you go
you are met with smiles whoever you meet
the moment you step into the country it feels like home

Our music will have you bobbing your head
the rhythm will bring out your inner dancer
It will bring joy to your heart
you won't want to leave

Where I am from is a place of resilient people
big hearts and strong characters
we may be knocked down- but marks my words
we will rise again

Dear Phone

I'm sorry to say that you aren't my first
that honour belongs to an old Sagem- or was it a Nokia?
It was too long ago I don't remember
they weren't special though- not like you are

You replaced my watch and my alarm
I never thanked you for that
we spend a lot of time together
you are my best friend
sad- I know
you know how to be silent when I want quiet time
you hear and see all my little secrets
that scares me sometimes

I know I neglect you sometimes
especially when your low battery light goes on
and I let you die

You may not be my first- but I treasure you all the same
you have my whole life in your hands
what would I do without you?

You have lost me a lot of time
had me glued to the screen till late
you have brought me laughs though
memorable phone calls that I won't ever forget
pings that came with bad and good news

Sometimes I want to switch you off and forget about you
I'm not saying I don't appreciate you though
hold on
I'm getting a call

Dear Food

We've been through a lot
you and I
I did the maths
you and I just don't add up anymore
that's just how it is

Our unhealthy relationship ends here
you have enabled me for far too long
especially when I am feeling vulnerable
I'm not blaming you

I blame myself for enjoying your company too much
I remember those sad days
I slept with you curled up next to me
I would wake up and you were nowhere to be found
now all I have to show for it are the extra kgs
well played

Dear Music

We spend hours together
without getting bored of each other
even when we spend days apart
we carry on like no time has passed

You bring joy to my heart
you feed my soul
because of you sometimes I break down in tears
then sometimes you make me laugh

When I'm alone you hug me with your sound
when my heart aches you heal me with your sweet melody
when I'm happy your rhythm runs through my veins
you silence the noise in my head

You are there for me whatever the time
you comfort me whatever the mood
you get me

Dear Crush

I love how your skin glows in the sun
In the right light your melanin looks like
it's coated with honey
the way your eyes smile when your teeth sparkle
Colgate better give you a call

The way your voice sounds like my favourite song
how it echoes in my heart when I think of you
my heart hums your name when you are near

Can you picture you and I hand in hand?
nothing but the birdsongs to keep us company
clear skies- walking under the jacaranda bloom

When I close my eyes
there you are lighting up my world again
I think of you- there goes that silly grin again
you just may be the key that unlocks my heart

Dear Mama

Where do I even start?
I don't know where I would be if I didn't
have you in my corner
I am the man I am today because of you

Thank you for never giving up on me
I am sorry I sometimes took you for granted

Your infectious laugh- I take after you
we can talk about anything and everything for hours
we have a code word for every situation
when we watch TV and something weird happens
we give each other 'the look'
there's one for every situation
when I was younger that look scared me
I knew when I was misbehaving- and you gave me 'the look'
trouble was brewing

You taught me to appreciate every blessing
you have always been my biggest fan
I pray God blesses you with a long life
I hope my daughter grows to be just as wonderful as you are
a loving woman- God fearing and of good character
you are my biggest blessing
I'm proud to be your son

Dear Future Daughter

I hope this finds you well
I hope to be the father you deserve

I will do my best to prepare myself for fatherhood
to give you a wonderful life
to prepare you for the world

You have many black Queens to look up to
to inspire you when you need it
to celebrate your every victory
to lift you up when you get knocked down

Be appreciative of those who appreciate you
give with your heart
don't be a prop in people's lives
If your heart is unsettled- remove yourself from the situation
build walls around what you hold dear

I hope to support your dreams in any way I can
to advise you about all life has to offer
I don't want you to make the same mistakes I did
I have had too many outtakes

I will be here when you need a shoulder to lean on
I will spoil you when I can
I will teach you how to be grateful for everything you have
to thank God for every blessing
to be a person of good character and to have a loving heart

I have no doubt you will be a wonderful woman
I can't wait to meet you

Dear Future Son

I hope this finds you well
I wonder what kind of man you will be
I hope I will be the father you deserve

God never gives you more than you can handle
trust in that and let it guide you in life
You will experience heartbreak- loss- rejection
don't let it harden your heart
keep going for what your heart desires
even if it scares you

Be appreciative of those who appreciate you
give with your heart
don't be a prop in people's lives
If your heart is unsettled- remove yourself from the situation
build walls around what you hold dear

I hope to support your dreams in any way I can
to advise you about all life has to offer
I don't want you to make the same mistakes I did
I have had too many outtakes

I will be here when you need a shoulder to lean on
I will spoil you when I can
I will teach you how to be grateful for everything you have
to thank God for every blessing
to be a person of good character and to have a loving heart

Be free to be whoever you want to be
be proud to be who you are
I can't wait to meet you

Fool

Little was said yet much was meant
out of nowhere you came like a Mediterranean breeze
brought me warmth and made me shiver

Memories of you are as clear as yesterday
my feelings are forever anchored to you
our passion was so strong it felt like magic
memories of you linger like tidewrack

We were like the sea and the pirate
you brought me sorrow along with joy
once upon a time we were a fairy-tale
unfortunately- a happy ever after is to mark an ending

Now that you are gone- I love the pain that you cause
maybe it's true- I am a fool

If I Were You

If I were you- I would hate me too
I was terribly unkind
what did you see in me?

In finding you- I found myself
you brought the best out of me
you were the best of me
you showed me what it's like to be loved
like a fool I took it for granted

At the first sign of trouble I walked away
I thought I was sparing you disappointment
I was not worthy of your love
pride got the best of me

We were great together- perfect even
that time I came to see you- your face was a picture
the sparkle in your eyes
I will forever treasure that

Precious moments we had plenty
we were happy and madly in love
I should have done better
Instead of finding a solution
I found an exit
I am not the man I thought I was

The one thing I promised to keep safe
I shattered to pieces

Heartache

Imagine feeling like you had the wind knocked out of you
like you are drowning on dry land
being strangled by the burdens of life

As if a dagger has pierced your heart
writhing on the ground as if
you have been punched in the unmentionables

Feeling an overwhelming urge to bawl-but
making no sound
trying to pull your hair out
but there's nothing to grasp

Kicking the air but gravity wins
hitting the ground and causing a tremor for the ants
you are out like a candle

I Loved You Once

I loved you once
then the storm came and took our love with it
left in its wake my shrivelled heart wasting away

We both lashed out unsavoury words
left in their wake an uneasy stench
the memories we made together are all but washed away
the cute trinkets we made for each other are meaningless now

Remember the first time we met?
that beautiful summer's day
your sparkling smile caught my eye
when our eyes met
I swear the world stopped for a moment

Where did it all go wrong?
we were head over heels for each other
you were my everything
one day you just up and leave
I hope you are happy wherever you are
Well- not really

Adulting

Remember when you had no worries about bills?
all you had to worry about was waking up- eating- living
sleep and repeat
well tough luck you are a grown up now

You bought a brand-new phone with your rent money
you scream into your pillow
no bank of mum and dad to bail you out
you did this to yourself all for a drop of clout
thanks to the pandemic that is fomo

You go on spending sprees like you're made of money
how will you pay off that credit card?
with your lotto winnings?
Okay then

How is that life plan going?
are you living large yet?
has that piece of paper made you rich yet?
Sorry- I meant your degree
how is that student debt treating you?
Have I hit a nerve?
my bad

Tirelessly working only to make ends meet
you can't afford to eat out anymore
why?
because there's food at home!

I Lost Myself

I lost myself along the way
I was idle while my mind was in decay
I had no idea who I was anymore
even the things I used to enjoy became a chore

My bed became my best friend
life became my nemesis
instead of living it I dreaded it

I kept the curtains drawn even when the sun was shining
instead of breathing the fresh air I stewed in my damp air
instead of embracing the light- I latched on to the dark

I left my bed only for food and to relieve myself
I gathered all my necessities close by
as if I was in hibernation

I was blind to my own self decay
Mind- body and spirit weakened with every sunset
I became sensitive to my feet hitting the ground
suffering from withdrawal if I was away
from my bed for too long
I craved my head being cradled by the pillow

As I lay in bed- I lost track of time
procrastination befriended me
the hours turned into days
with each sunset I became a shadow of my former self

Former Self

The carcass of my former self burns away
the debris clings on for dear life
self-pity slowly gnaws at my sanity

I lose myself in the journey- destination unknown
I can't close my eyes
I fear what rabbit hole my mind will drag me down

A plastered smile covers the discord in my heart
I dance in the rain to hide my tears
the mask I wear- clings on like a leech

Dear You

Hey you
I wish you knew your worth
maybe then you would stop wasting time
on the wrong people
Guard your heart
don't always wear your heart like a bracelet

Whatever you dream of- follow through
don't be a master of half measures
complete what you start

Be careful about who you let into your life
there are people who want to see you fail at life
they don't know what you have been through
to get where you are
don't take it for granted
don't live to satisfy people's expectations either
live to fulfil your potential

Look in the mirror and look hard
that there is a warrior
you are no fool
stop acting like one

Remember to take good care of yourself
learn new languages- skills- meet new people
and explore the world
don't exist in a bubble
Be someone worth remembering

In Silence

Something is gnawing at your mind
you grin and bear it
you lock it away and keep going

Out of nowhere you have an outburst
you fall on your knees
tears stream down your cheeks
you are overwhelmed

The boiling pot that is your heart is bubbling over
it spills all over the place
the 'Wet floor' sign comes out
everyone must tread carefully
they don't know what will trigger you

It was bound to happen
you never dealt with what was weighing on your heart
you thought it best to suffer in silence

Survival

Smack dab in the middle of nowhere
I'm lost
I'm a castaway
I scream but the forest answers me with echoes
the sea drowns my voice

Survival is my only burden
If only I can conjure my inner Bear Grylls
If only I wasn't so domesticated

Nothing but my wits to survive
as the light descends my fear heightens
strange sounds in the distance
I doubt I will sleep sound

Listen

Listen- what you are feeling right now
it gets better
I won't lie to you and say it will completely go away
you learn to live with it
and move on with your life
there will be reminders of the past everywhere
learn to be at peace with it
the nightmares will pass
there are moments you find yourself tearing up
Well- you aren't a robot

Never Forgotten

Losing a loved one brings unmeasurable pain
knowing you will only see their face on pics and videos
hearing their voice through voice notes only

How you smile when you think of them
only to start crying when you remember
everything they've missed out on
and everything they will miss out on
birthdays
graduations
weddings
family gatherings

You are grateful for the memories
their quirks
how they made you smile
the selfies
the shared laughs
the tears too

You do your best to make sure their memories live on
and that the younger generation learn about them
how funny they were
their compassion
their presence
their kind hearts
you make sure they are never forgotten

Dear Uncle

There is a lot I wish I could have told you
you were taken from us too soon
then again- is there ever a good time?

I looked up to you
I had no words for Maiguru and my cousins- just hugs
I'm grateful we got to bond
I will always treasure the time you told me
all about the family tree
we drove around listening to the reggae tunes
you used to listen to with Dad
you told me the stories of your Djing days- 'Jah Simplicity'

That time the tyre burst when we were out for a drive
we had to change it in the pouring rain
thanks to the good Samaritans who assisted us
we joked about the potholes that have riddled our roads

we sat in your garage and we shared beers and stories
I wish I had known we wouldn't get another chance
to have a drink together
I would have made sure we took
plenty of selfies to cement the moments
I am grateful we got the chance to bond

We didn't always talk
I regret that
I pray God continues to comfort Maiguru and my cousins

The family tree remains unfinished
you put so much work into it
I will make sure we finish it in your honour

Dear Sekuru

I will miss your words of wisdom
I will miss our calls
especially talking about your garden
all the crops you had planted for that season
I enjoyed making lists of the seeds and equipment
you needed for your garden
I always looked forward to bringing them whenever I visited

I will miss banging the chain against the gate
to say I've arrived
also- just in case the dogs came running after me
the warm welcome from you
"Hello Muzukuru"- you would say

Walking into house my heart would smile
you would sit on your favourite sofa- your phone by your side
your diary- glasses- hat and newspaper
we would regale each other with stories
while sipping on some tea and biscuits

The tour around the garden would be glorious
I loved how your face would light up
when talking about your garden
the garden always looked vibrant
with plenty of fruits and vegetables
the beautiful blooming flowers
the way the juicy plums and guavas glistened under the sun
No wonder you won all those awards at the agricultural show

Whenever your name is mentioned it's with great admiration
you brought incomparable joy into our lives
you were truly an inspiration